SALT

_____

The Brittingham Prize in Poetry

The University of Wisconsin Press Poetry Series
Ronald Wallace, General Editor

Places/Everyone • Jim Daniels
C. K. Williams, Judge, 1985

Talking to Strangers • Patricia Dobler
Maxine Kumin, Judge, 1986

Saving the Young Men of Vienna • David Kirby
Mona Van Duyn, Judge, 1987

Pocket Sundial • Lisa Zeidner
Charles Wright, Judge, 1988

Slow Joy • Stefanie Marlis
Gerald Stern, Judge, 1989

Level Green • Judith Vollmer
Mary Oliver, Judge, 1990

Salt • Renée Ashley
Donald Finkel, Judge, 1991

Renée Ashley

SALT

The University of Wisconsin Press

The University of Wisconsin Press
114 North Murray Street
Madison, Wisconsin 53715

3 Henrietta Street
London WC2E 8LU, England

5 4 3 2 1

Printed in the United States of America

Library of Congress Cataloging-in-Publication Data
Ashley, Renée.
    Salt / Renée Ashley.
    70 pp.   cm. — (The Brittingham prize in poetry)
    ISBN 0-299-13140-8   ISBN 0-299-13144-0
    I. Title.   II. Series.
    PS3551.S387S25   1991
    811'.54—dc20   91-12357
                        CIP

For Jack

CONTENTS

ACKNOWLEDGMENTS

Grateful acknowledgment is made to the editors of the following publications in which these poems first appeared:

Bird Watcher's Digest: "Crow"
California Quarterly: "Laurel"
Creeping Bent: "February, 4 P.M."
The Greensboro Review: "Wild Radish"
Iris: A Journal About Women: "The Way Women Sweat"
The Kenyon Review: "Salt"
Mid-American Review: "Not the First Snow"
The Nebraska Review: "The Light at My Father's House," and "Wishbone"
Oxalis: "The Dream I Don't Remember"
Passaic County Community College Poetry Center Contest Anthology:
    "Photograph, 1962"
South Coast Poetry Journal: "Burning the Sheets"
Southern Poetry Review: "The Last Night You Are Gone," "The Hyacinth
    Bowl," and "Warrington Ave."
Widener Review: "East"

I wish to express my gratitude to the New Jersey State Council on the Arts for a Fellowship which made the writing of some of the poems in this volume possible. I would also like to acknowledge several awards. "Crow" was awarded the 1986 Washington Prize in Poetry by Word Works Inc., Washington, D.C.; "The Light at My Father's House" was the 1987 Ruth Lake Memorial Award winner from the Poetry Society of America; and "Salt" was co-recipient of the Robert H. Winner Memorial Award, Poetry Society of America, 1989, winner of the 1989 Open Voice Award, Writer's Voice, West Side Y, New York, and the Second Annual *Kenyon Review* Award for Literary Excellence for Emerging Writers.

Special thanks to Brigit Pegeen Kelly and Michael Madonick for their patience and generosity, and to Jack Pirkey for his support and understanding.

I

Warrington Ave.

Rita's house was yellow tin,
and small, east of ours, and closer
to the corner store, the penny candy, the bar,
and the place lost dogs hung out. And
by the westbound highway, Cristofani
built a white stucco mastodon of a house
—black bars on the windows, and granite steps
like a Bridge of Sighs to the red
double-thick door no 'piss-assed
young punk' would dare kick in. Our

lot on Warrington was ludicrously
large for a city mother, my mover-on
father, half a fertile acre caught
between the junkyard and the wrecker,
and right across the tar-patched road
from crazy MacRoy, his lean-to shack,
and the fat plumber in a duplex
who kept young girls. And out of the flat

brown dirt behind our house, lettuce grew,
and apricots, and the mud got shin-deep,
and the waist-high weeds were full of bugs,
and out past my father's for-stew rabbits,
around my mother's tin-voiced
chickens, was the junkyard
and the wrecking yard
and the mean brown dog called "Botts"
who, on my mother's oath, could peck, like a bird,
the eyes from a child who got too near
the fence—heavy-gauge, insinuating, crowned
by barbed wire, and taller than me by seven heads.
They made me swear I would not touch
that fence. But, every chance

I got, I did. And the oily men
behind the rusted cars, in over-
alls like greasy bags, and skinny
pegged-jeaned boys digging through the open maws
of decomposing Studebakers, Nashes with the seats
laid back, and Pontiacs for parts, would say:

> Hey, girlie-girlie, watch
> your fingers in the wire,

and

> Where's your mother, honey?
> Where's your mother?

and the mean brown dog would wag his tail,
and for as long as I would stand
and watch, for each one who said 'shit'
or 'watch who you're fuckin' with, you stupid
son-of-a-bitch,' another would 'shhhh'
and point his black or blackened
finger at me, looking through
and holding on the eyes and mouth
of that relentless fence.

My Mother Skating

I picture the steepest street in San Francisco
and I put her there, all obtuse angles, elbows

and hips, and lean as a poor cut of meat—my mother,
roller-skating back up the hill. The way she tells it,

she had a date and an hour to kill, so she pulled her skates
from beneath her narrow bed and, at home on the wild

precipitous streets, she played. I imagine the places
where her bones came together, her joints working

hard, pumping those wheels hard to gain the hill
when she remembered him, the skirt of her striped dress

bellowed back between her knees, full between the bare legs.
He was a dazzler, from a family of dazzlers; he came to her,

hands filled with chips of ice, the gift the girl would like,
the gift he could afford. She says, at thirty he trailed water

behind him, as later in his life he would trail urine
and bad news. Yet he waited in the full sun

for her, waited while she totted up miles on the pitted wheels;
he gave her more ice in a day than she could suck in her life,

and she took it—she was so taken, herself, by the older man,
by his sad history of love, the taste of which was clear

and good in her mouth, fresh as the ice he gave her.
They both drank it in and the pattern of sadness

built around them, as the callus had built on her heel
where the skate attached to her shoe. And she asked him

to wait while she drew the key from her dress, blind
to the layer of sweat at the neckline where the full breasts

topped the slight body. Facile as thread, she begged
forgiveness while she pulled off her skates and ran

up the stairs, for the transformation, for the woman she kept
in her one good dress, in her stockings, and her box

of dime-store mascara. She was as blind
to her own charm, to the mind of the ripe girl,

as she was to the sway of her breasts beneath her dress,
and to the sorrow, imprinted somewhere deep and near her heart,

blind to the inevitability of unhappiness stamped
on her genes, passed like ice from mouth to thirsty mouth.

Wild Radish

Most weeds show little variety; wild radishes are an
exception because no one plant typifies the species. Wild
radish flowers blooming in the same field often vary in
hue, shape, and even vein color.
—Norman C. Ellstrand, *Natural History*, October 1985

In October, the first day I sense the Eastern sun is mine
(my nature having taken the turn
               —one hundred and eighty degrees out—)
I am resigned, and loving it, to an ocean
          on the wrong side.

On the second of Jersey porches, lobbed by delight
               into my favorite Salvation
               Army chair, I read, the pages
               slick and heavy in my hands
and my eyes glaze with the thought
of wild radish in the vacant lot
               behind the school in the poorer part
               of that California town,
radish grown wild with the mustard, so far
               from the jungle gym
               the chalkboard dust
(well within sight of monitors and mothers
        if they cared to watch
        —they seldom did).
It took no time to get there, no time to return
And recess, like a dash between solar systems,
        was the sound of petals
        whispering our names.

No one plant, the article says, *typifies the species.*
(The photo is a paint-spatter
                    all wild radish.
All the colors there, sprouting like cowlicks
            amidst the insane yellow of the mustard.)
I know now that's what it was
                    out there behind the school.

I read: *multiple paternity*
                    multi-
                            seeded
                                    pods
                    leaf shape, texture, mother
                    father
                    pink, purple, bronze, brick

And I smell the sweet-sour
        juice that rose under our feet
stained white Keds piss-green
And the others, the ticklers, felt
                beneath layers
                of anomalous, even-at-the-time foolish
                petticoats.

The words form loments on my tongue: *parent*
                                    progeny
                                    allo-
                                            zyme.

It is in the genes. Pollen
    like dusty semen
    spread by the ankles of insects,
    seeds by the wind or the hem of a skirt,
                genetic dexterity
                to the *nth* degree
and still a weed.

And though I sit content as cream, though here
    leaves dangle from trees,
flounce downward with flair and hide whatever's left
    of any old summer
though they turn or stay
    with great and studied regularity:
        grass green, sea green, celadon like glass
    some topaz,
        amber, carnelian, cinnabar, clay
though some few redder than any child's blood
I find that I could bear
        the ocean on the other side
        the rampant promis-
            cuity
            of more familiar ground
and the staggering unpredictability
of wild radish.

The Dream I Don't Remember

In the dream I don't remember, my father
waltzes me on shoes, steel-toed, black

and shiny as licorice. There is a white
dress of something sheer, and white gathered

petticoats crisp as paper, two of them,
or three, flinging their weightless selves out, one

over the other, billowing like an open parachute,
out from the shapeless white body, the precarious child;

we dance though there is no music, only the dark
green-painted concrete floor, only the pale green

walls, the single curtainless window,
dusty as a desert, the color of sand. There is no sound,

no door, we have no eyes, no memories, we choose
to have no mouths, and there is no lover,

no bottle of port behind the workbench wall, no pale
mother, no time, just two figures dancing, no thoughts

of a woman at all, just a small girl's white-stockinged feet
clinging like wild things to a father's shoes.

The Hyacinth Bowl

I

The four lean poplars fragment the light, strew it,
    stingy and broken
against the upper story pane, through the dust
    carried from the schoolyard

and the unkempt fields beyond the wooden fences,
    to the gray-green walls,
to our faces when we pass through its sallow trajectory.
    Some occasion, some

obvious, overt apology from a dialogue I missed,
    has left, like a promise,
a dry purple bulb in an hourglass bell,
    mouth wide as a fist, silent as no mouth,

swirling up like a galaxy from the polished wood
    of my mother's dressing table
—as though the glass itself, early in its liquid life,
    had been stirred quickly,

drawn upwards, and left. Even the fulvous dampered light
    lets the still glass mouth spin
and the rootless bulb rests, concentric, its oniony core
    like an eye

in the center of another eye. Even I know the bulb
    must be enough;
we are the women and content to wait
    for the hyacinth.

II

Centered in the eddy of Italian glass, the bulb
    throws up a gawky wand

of stiff pink horns; rich as oil on the lip, waxy foliage
      rises like a lithe

green limb from the purple onion of a heart,
      and the sigh is neither mine
nor my mother's, but perhaps the dry wind
      taking the poplar leaves, spreading them

brown and deep beneath the windows; for the first time
      I question
the sex of flowers, and this single bulb stranded
      in its deliberate glass,

flowering—how some are set by ordinary hands to water
      and some to dirt,
how some thrive for their given time, how some,
      lifeless in their papery skins, never do.

III

The light falls between the poplars and then again
      on his familiar arm,
the long black hairs that cover the length
      to the elbow, the yellow nails

like yellow hooves, ridged, uneven at the fingertip;
      his white-hot 'goddamns'
mix with the too-thick air of the too-small room,
      the smell of sweat and tepid

water, the broken glass, bent stalk, a fistful
      of sorry, browning blossoms,
his lacerated hand, the cut itself, the blood,
      red-black and thick like molasses

on the glass shards smaller than seeds on the carpet.
      The smell of warm urine sours,
stirred up with the old odor of wine. We are voiceless
      and deaf; we gather debris

—we cup our hands, ourselves the receptacles,
    we wrench splinters from the selvedge of the rug,
swab the wall, the darkened, wetted paint where the glass
    broke apart, and pick up the recognizable

pieces; we gather in our hands the thin, convex sides,
    the uneven remnants
of the cinched glass neck, the solemn 'oh'
    of its delicate, twisted mouth.

The Way Birds Must Live

Today, a snow as fine as salt
        sparse and invisible, and until it gathers
more silent than breath on the stones
        on the woods, it is nothing in the air
a mist, the slightest of shadows.

The only moving thing is the perfect fox sparrow
        fat and marbled, bellowed up against the cold
and choosy at his seed; he ignores the suet
        the halved orange. He keeps his wide eyes down
to the ground where squirrels have broadcast

what the feeder held before; he listens for the dogs
        and does not hear them. Only the English
sparrow, the wounded one, scarred on her right
        bare cheek, featherless and healed,
only she utters the sound of coming and then

lands the awkward landing of the injured, old
        injury, old pain. She shows no fear, but regard;
she tastes suet and picks the cleanest seed from near
        her brother bird's feet; together they share
the generosity of plenty. She is his other, his smaller

self, aware of but indifferent to this slight snow, alive
        with not knowing and then with nearly
understanding, their mostly silent exchange, this implausible
        maneuver. She is to him what matters most
in his life: a reminder of the way birds must live.

The Light at My Father's House

Sometimes I hear the light falling
through the redwoods, sifting down,

always the upright shafts of light,
the sound like constant rain. The door

to my father's house is closed, brittle
door, old cabin cantilevered off its own

mountainside twenty-five years and three
thousand miles ago—two wooden rooms,

pullman-like and warm, the big stone
hearth and mantel mortared in place

in my mind, the house itself tethered
to the upraised earth as if by cobwebs,

blue before they were invisible, tatted
at the corners of the dark split shingles

a strange lace mysterious as the edges
of my grandmother's hankies. Impossible

to leave behind: the smell of unceasing shadow,
of water underground, and a forest floor breathing,

the hush like sheep's wool beneath my shoes,
and no sun, no sun but the faintest strands

of hazy light between the redwoods, always
the vertical, splendid light between the trees.

II

If he was expecting me, he'd make chili
and cake, the clang of red pepper riding along-

side the sweet scent of apples in his kitchen
—the port wine hidden, the overwhelming antiseptic

presence of lysol in the john, the house all dusted
and dress-up-like-Sunday clean, even my sleeping bag

beaten with a broom and hung on the rail
like a flayed skin to air. And after hello, a walk

up the steep hill behind the house, up in the half-dark
to see the bark wind itself off the spools of trunks,

parchment the color of dried blood, the red of madrone
dying our hands deep brown where we touched it, turning

them finally black; stubborn like pitch, it had to wear
off. And if it was summer, and if I could stay,

in the morning I'd walk to the dam and the sand
where I'd burn my radish-white skin so red

I'd have to sleep on wet towels and drink
my father's beer for fear of drying out

and dying there. And each night, simply
because I liked it, no matter what heat still

clung to my father's narrow rooms, he'd make a show
of splitting wood, kindle and stack the grate

so that crazy fire would climb way up
inside the flue and I'd lie close on the floor,

read by the wavering light, and sweat, my father
silent in the background reading too,

knowing time was short, knowing the outside world
was silenced by humus deep as my arm was long:

acid and heat, a deeper roiling than hell.
Knowing creatures smaller and stronger,

wilier than ourselves, called that night
home, and knowing we could not, we tried to force

the light to stay, to make our lives over, all over
again—trying to make them come out right, we read,

instinctive as animals inside our skins,
we said nothing, confided nothing.

III

Here, where the Jersey flatlands flood each spring
without fail, where Doty's Point goes under

and the geese swim the length of the bridge,
a heavy light is broadcast, as dull and gray

as the ragged squirrels that run down my oaks
like water. I think about the six black

cats my father had, his bringing them home
like quarts of milk, one after the other,

small thin cats named Blackie, a string
of Blackies. And when the Ramapo rises

and the rain falls heavy as a sheet of glass
I can't help but see redwoods

and bridges washed like gravel
from those California mountains, people and houses

stripped away by rains and the San Lorenzo
clearing the land. My mother sent the clipping:

the house in the *Tribune* could have been my father's,
given away, two decades ago, for taxes, to a priest

from the suburbs who planned to raise
a crop of boys like corn or wheat

there where the trees made the heat more
bearable. And even with that black and white opened

sky, a striated light hung over the house, over the rising
water, as though the trees had left their imprint

on the air, light still coming in bands, somehow
sensing the importance of shape, and falling

on the cat, one black and terrified
cat on the roof as the peak went under

a small cat, thin with fear, caught
forever going down.

The Song the Rocks Make

Listen: the sound like wood on wood, the song
The rocks make. It is everywhere up and down

This sopping road: the hollow beating of heartwood,
The stone throbbing. It is the thaw

Running through the mountain like breath—it bleats like sheep
In the thin tracks beneath my skin. Stark

Forsythia bears the wetting bud, but even the dogs
Still think winter is all there is: running,

They keep to the center, the gravelly strip the plow
Might have cleared. But the rocks that are the mountain

Sweat; even on the sunless side they open their slaggy mouths
And sing *fresh* and *moss clear as the eye of god.* Listen:

The sound like wood on wood, the song the rocks make.

Hillview

Nothing changes in the mind:
Think about the concrete slab
　　　Where the apricots dropped. Think
About the fence: the grapestake,

　　　The drunken carpenter who played
Your guitar. Think about the time
　　　You turned the kitchen black with hot
Grease, think about the sirens

　　　And the sober firemen; think
About the insane mockingbird
　　　That lived over your garage.
Remember when your mother bought the house, remember

　　　That it listed eastward: one
Enormous swell rolling to the rear. The furnace
　　　Blew cold air. Think about the drive,
And the crack so wide you nearly expected

　　　A full-blown palm to rise from the string
Of weeds there. Picture the rain pools, your mother
　　　Under the house and on her knees bailing sewage:
Terra cotta pipe *infirma*, the obvious resurrection.

　　　Think about the salamanders, the smell of mildew
Rising like the long dead wafting homeward,
　　　Heavenward, up to the soles of God's feet.
Think about God's feet. When the man next door

　　　Died, the whole world went to hell: his wife,
His vine-woven arbor, his big green car. The grapes
　　　Dried up; his apples got worms. The crazy Lithuanian
Whore on the corner got crazier: no more old man

Giving her the waspy eye. Think about an old man's
Eye. If you want, think about the gunshot;
     Think about your father, another old man, shooting
The gun. Think about the wall he hit. Then, remember

     The spring Frankie planted radishes, remember
Your mother's wild-eyed marguerites spreading like crabgrass
     In the lava-dry soil. Think about the dogs thinking
About the mockingbird. Picture Hillview, as good

     As its name, all changed, all the same. Picture the Easter
Cross high on the mountain big as a dream, recall the fog,
     Voluminous, opaque as blindness spreading over the hills.
Picture the tule low as macadam. Think about who's

     Still there, who might be, who isn't. Think about change
In the mind and out. Think about mockingbirds and change.

II

The Animals Below

It was never just the animals:
   it was your opossum aunt strung
with her ridiculous Paris silk scarves,
   it was the balloon man with the mustache
thick as bear fur, then it was the dog
   who followed you home, the gray dog who looked
like the sorry mutt that followed your father
   home, the dog with the one blank eye that roamed
the way your teacher's eye drifted left
   when you were ten, and wild with impatience, always
left, towards the window, the ravaged poplar,
   the wasps' nests—you would have gone with it
if you could. No, it was never just
   the animals. Somewhere in keeping track,
the lines got crossed; the hybrid species
   that is your mind confused you, addled your
perceptions. No wonder you don't know
   the difference. Look, the way I see it,
out there it's only faces—and when God
   runs out of faces He repeats Himself.
That woman in Reno who, unequivocally,
   is not your chinless coast-of-France aunt,
is so like her she should be; there she is,
   your sliver-faced aunt, three-dimensional and
smelling of the sea, ready with the others,
   your past and your future, in your mind.
You see, God's got this funny sense
   of humor. It's all the same to Him:
three orange cats in heat, six bankers, a lost
   dog, your opossum aunt, the animals below.

Crow

At dusk, the flat lake, blacker
than a crow's wing, is still.
It bargains with the hills

for the last blue hour. Our pines
harbor three invisible birds; their voices
are the voices of the half-night.

There is no impasse at dark, only
the slow change to some other thing,
some other time when the currency

of light is valueless and gem-eyed
mammals scour the hedges for food.
At midnight, the long-eared owl will call

from the pitch pine, call plainly
for what he knows is his. The whisper of tree
and wing and fur is fate.

We have not the eyes for darkness
and our ears are poor cousins
to those who measure the night. We

are the pale ones, the sleeping ones,
who, when the black crow cries
his alarum, rise feebly and face the light.

East

In the East,
there is the change of clothes to think about
like the changing of some guard:

That day when all the winter
bunting's shuffled down the basement stairs
gray-brown rag wool scratch, invisible
           miracle-insulate draw-
           string gear like Grandma
           never had
hung or folded, shelved, drawered
mothballed, stashed
           in the dark
like the grave-flag of some navy father,
a crisp-edged
           and thick three-corner thought:

        that first snow day you lost your gloves
        and in looking found the birds, junco, white-
           throated sparrow,
        at the feed tray you'd set out and filled
           just that morning.
        You believed
        they counted on your seeds
        and crumbs.

Then sit upstairs, bare-armed, open-handed
over tea, and out the window clear as summer
two bees
like bumbling hippos poise
black as tar, yellow as burst
           —forsythia—
humming like fat Gods
a bladdernut hymn

And the washed-soft cotton of the careless
                    yellow blouse
dug this morning from dark drawer,
drawn over pale shoulders,
lies like brushed pollen
on your skin.

Wishbone

Split around Slocum Pond
the mud road at night
drags like the tail
of a comet, long about
the frozen edge, longer
than in the day.

There is little to gauge by.
The water's crust is swallowed
by the moon; that shallow light
is doubled then, and your ear
sharpened by the dark. The crack
of a twig is ice beneath your feet.
It bends your breath back on you
and the clear melon light, hard
against your unaccustomed eye, wavers
in response. The smell of night
and ice is strong.

When you walk there
sound is without reason:
the cat's foot is stronger
than the camel's in the dark,
the rodent's is a man's at least.
In my walking shoes, I am
Bigfoot or a backhoe treading
the crisp dirt around the ledge,
the lake's border like lace
risen up in the freeze.

If the owls are out,
you feel smaller.
Their hollow sighs alone
eclipse your thoughts
and you hear only your breast-
bone, your wishbone,
the tympan of your heart
at your tongue.

February, 4 P.M.

At four o'clock, three brown dogs
of varying hues reach the high notes,
and the gold sun swells, throbs
like a heartbeat through the double glass,

and, as though I have eyes, eyes but no lids,
there is no looking away. In sixty minutes,
the reservoir, thick and flat as silvered glass,

will go gray cold and still. This same sun grew
softly over our sky, around the low brush, quiet
as ice, quiet as still snow, moved with no wings,
moved like an avatar; and now, from this chair

I seem to never leave, it is as cruel to the eyes,
as difficult to look upon, as the godhead; now
it is a platinum sky, and, soon, that slender
western slice over the water is the luminous

flesh of salmon, then bluer, blue as aubergine,
then black as the eye of a crow. The sky, tableau
vivant, will give the appearance of being still,
then lower itself quickly, like a cruel cat.

I will watch one hot star flicker, then drop
the blinds, and wait for you.

Laurel

It is barely light. We are late for work, we are always late
for work. The plow does its poor-shave job, but still from
front door to car, car to road, the snow is mid-shin and
clean; it makes the bones to the knee hum with cold. We
will try to get out without shoveling behind the car. We
will fail.

The jay in the laurel throws out a croak like a gold coin.
The weak light catches on the leather-green leaves,
glances off the wiry wood, sends shadows down like more
snow, and the jay, fat as a ham hock in there, waits

for us, then, in a huff, launches himself into the branches
of a bare oak, high, over our bent heads; he preens a wing
and sends out the news of how we would not see. Like
something unrelated, we hear the sigh of the new sun
on the snow crust. The whisper is like a ghost dancing
at our ears.

Burning the Sheets

We cut the jonquils and the daffodils,
    steeped their raw stems in the cold tea and wrapped
        them in paper; carefully we laid the bunches

on the seats of our separate cars. You packed
    the cups and the old gray towels—working
        from the outside in, we stripped the house

of the last of ourselves. Each of us knew the lesson
    by heart: when it gets down to it, you're alone. So
        we burned the sheets on the lawn; still

damp from the last sex, they smouldered,
    a slow erratic burning, black fragments moving upward
        from the slight, unsuitable fire. We watched

then turned our backs. The sparse smoke drifted
    to the open cars and lowered itself like a single, dazed lover
        on the brash yellow flowers waiting in the sun.

Not the First Snow

The smallest pines are folded
nearly double and pale brown doves
hobble across the frozen ground

as if their feet are bound. Their thumbnail
heads bob and jut like weak fingers desperate
to make a point, any point; their blind gourd

bodies follow behind. There is no trace
of wind; the heavy snow lies still
on the narrowest of gray branches and does

not fall. Two titmice, ruddy-haunched and quicker
than their brothers, squeak the feeder clean,
and the body heat of squirrels clears the ground

of snow below. It is not the first snow,
yet, in the withered azalea, stubborn blossoms blink rose-
colored eyes from underneath, and the small blond boy

across the road, squeals and slides
down the hillock on a garbage bag, still awed
by the whiteness and the wetness of it all, all around.

The Way Women Sweat

"Ladies don't sweat, dear. They glow."
—Mother

Glow, my ass. Women sweat
wet as the tongues of dogs,
wildly slick beneath the breasts, beneath
the arms the body's water,
the body's salts like an oily sea;
and, where the soft thighs part at the open
mouth of the sex, where the dusky
flesh smothers, raw as an oyster, slick
as a throat, and bright like pearl or shell
in the dark, the musty smell of rich effluvium
lingers like air heavy with pollen and heat.

The Last Night You Are Gone

The dogs
are wild
with loneliness.
From the hallway
where the light
burned out
four days ago,
the bed
looks as long
and unpeopled
as Interstate 80,
at Rawlins,
the time
we came
East
and were
stranded
in the storm.

I sleep
on the couch
the last night
you are gone
as if sleeping
with the dogs
in an unaccustomed
place without you
would bring
us close,
but each car
that goes by,
invisible
in the dark,

makes the dogs go
crazy and they leap
to greet you
all night
long; no one
sleeps. My job
is to tell them,
over and over, you
are not coming.

By tomorrow
we'll braid ourselves
together, leg
thrown to hip,
arm to the crown
of the head,
a lazy knot
of comfortable
indifferent body

and be glad.
The dogs will lie
in dark masses
on the dark floor;
they'll see you
back, know
nothing changed
for good. They
only knew
you were
missing, knew
you were gone.
In their sadness,
they howled
like black
shadows of dogs
against a too bright
moon.

Skunk

We three just getting down getting naked when
     we gotta stop what we doing
'cause of the ruckus   something scared the hens off
     quick   we heard'm flapping like hell
and we looked out the window to see
     what the goddamn fuss was   thinking
it's that skinny gray
     tabby again   but no
it's a goddamn
     skunk and ain't we surprised

     and them dogs go crazy   'spite
of no cat
     yeah they go
wild to begin with 'cause
     what they figured was cat ain't
and so them dogs is barking
     wacko like mad and scratching
hell outta the screens and that skunk
     ain't dead   deaf   or blind yet
and we know we're gonna
     get skunked   oh boy
we're gonna get skunked good.

Then Boxy Widdens   he's new at the factory
     (and don't ever let no one tell you
lunchtime in a whorehouse gives you time
     for no sandwich)
well Boxy's got eyes like boiled
     eggs   and stutterin' says   it's
rabid   just look at its mouth   he keeps
     yelling   look at its god
damn mouth   but it ain't the mouth interests

me and I'm trying to shut them windows
and not scare the skunk
       at the same time into skunking.

Peter Hazey, who seen it all before, says   oh, shit,
       get out them cans of goddamn tomata
juice cause it's coming   but it still don't come
       and the skunk's looking both p.o.'d and tired
into the window
       all at the same time   just standing there
with its neck all turned   at us   when we think
       it's gonna turn back   and skunk
somebody else   instead it just falls
       where it is   and dies   maybe.

Now who's gonna poke it   Boxy wants to know   I
       ain't gonna
poke it he says   my luck it ain't died   't all
       just waiting
for me personally so's I can be the one gets
       skunked
and Peter Hazey shakes his head and says   Boxy's
       gone fruit loops and who's
gonna skunk somethin' like him on account of that boy
       already smells
worse'n the skunk and the skunk's probably scared
       shitless Boxy's
gonna skunk him   that's what probably
       paralyzed him he says.

So by now the dogs is watching Peter Hazey
       and Boxy go for
the throat but I'm watching the skunk which still
       ain't moved but I do get the windows
down just in time for Peter Hazey
       to knock Boxy through the big one
and land him in the huge red

berry bush which sticks him like
hell   and then there's Boxy
      in the spiny bush not knowing whether to yell
about the busted glass or the pricking
      or to shut up an' pray the skunk gonna
lay there still dead
      which he is still doing up 'til now.

So Peter Hazey's feeling pretty spunko
      and he figures he's got both
Boxy and the skunk quartered up so he goes
      stepping out the door to get Boxy
outta the bush an he's pulling
      on his collar when
that skunk rises
      up and skunks the shit outta both them men
and I quick
      close the door so it don't get
in no more'n has to   and already the dogs
      is howling and scraping their noses
and it's left to me
      to nail the one clean sheet up over
the busted window glass and
      to open them cans of tomata juice.

      But God he got one sense
of humor so when the Preacher Burker comes
      strollin' down the road here's naked Peter Hazey
shovelin' up this twice
      dead skunk and Boxy   who's out behind the tree
line burying those clothes   ain't
      nowhere to be seen just yet   and the Preacher says
Peter Hazey   what you doin' man?
      (Peter Hazey always said Preacher got no
sense of smellin'   says too many skunks
      on them parish rolls killed his smeller
an' he must of had it right)   anyway Preacher

                 says to Peter Hazey
you ain't got no clothes on, man
        and I can hear the two of 'em through
them closed windows and the one clean sheet.

Now it ain't like Preacher hisself ain't
        been here naked for quarter hour
or more   more'n once   so Preacher may not smell
        but he ain't dead to how we earns
our living   and even God believes
        in making a living with what you
got   so he's more curious why Peter Hazey's
        being naked on the outside not
the inside and why he's out there by hisself   so
        them preachery oggle-eyes is looking
wide for me   and then here comes Boxy dead raw
        'round from the rear and what Preacher
figures he's got here is trouble   so suddenly he gets
        the righteous blindness and he's walking
like God's on his behind.

Now I ain't begging trouble but
        I figures what comes is what
goes   and Boxy he says later   there's a goddamn
        moral in this thing   so I thinks yeah what's lost
is what's lost and that boy's business is good
        and gone   and three weeks later Preacher
he still laughing and since then there been
        two real fine sermons on Man's Nature and How
Sin Comes Courtin' in the Devil's Clothes
                and when I goes
out that gawd-awful blonde-headed Mary MacElroy working
        in the food store says to me:

what you doing, honey?   opening yourself
        up a diner?   and she's patting them replacement cans
of tomata juice like they's little tin heads

and I tells her right off
God don't play favorites,
    honey   I just look at her and I says right back
straight as I will   tomata juice cuts the smell,
    and you in your line and me in mine,
well, shit, Mary MacElroy, we all in this
    together and you probably ought to know
a little skunkin' ain't the big thing, no, no matter
    what you selling, honey
what comes is what's gonna go.

III

Why I Never Came
(Apology to My Mother)

I was nineteen, and that weekend I took
your old Chevrolet to the coast where I goaded
my sometimes lover, the one who put gin
in his coffee, into beating me. His fists
came like hammers, Mama, and when
he had worn himself out on me, when he dragged me
down the gravel road, I thought of you,
and when he laid me like a carcass
in the high grass at the side of Highway 1,
and the sea beat a hundred yards away, inseparable
from the throb of my body,
I thought of you then, too

but I did not come—you in the hospital
dying and I did not come. I bandaged
the ragged cut that swelled like an open mouth
over my eye and I did not come.
I could not say: Mama, I am my father's
daughter, or Mama, I earn beatings
the way you earn wages. I remember

the moon that night rose slowly and hung
large and gibbous over the hills, over
the roof of the hospital and I watched it
from the front steps of your house until dawn.

Places Behind the Eye

Sometimes you'll be eating grape-
        fruit at breakfast and the world
will flash—like something out of LSD
        —to a place behind the eye, a place
like a different life but not, a picture
        that's really just another part
of your own bigger picture. You don't
        have to be thinking about it.
It's as though the place has a mind
        of its own beyond yours, a real
electricity it uses to propel itself
        through space, uses to usurp
at will whatever landscape you own now.
        You'll be sitting there,
spitting out seeds, staring at the bill
        from the dentist, and all of a sudden
you're at the Palace of Fine Arts, a place
        you never visited much, just once
or twice, yet those damn big San Francisco swans
        hiss real close to your behind;
or, your feet will be in the ocean, that other
        ocean, numb from the cold, kicking off
loops of seaweed. There'll be black sand
        in your wine and you'll be alone. You get no
warning; as quick as light you're there
        and back, wondering how that happened,
wondering why. It's those places behind
        the eye, ingrained back there,
flaring up like a sort of spontaneous
        combustion, an internal explosion
of some small gray retentive cell which resents
        the opprobrium of time.

Assembly of God

Mother slept like wood, the congregation
gathering without me, coming together

without me. I shook the branches of her arms
and the slow fruit of her eyes took me in.

She moved like wood—every quarter hour
lengthened to what seemed like two or ten or twenty

quarter hours and still my sleepy mother
would not come downstairs, not drive the silver Chevy

to the Assembly of God and leave me there.

                                      Oh,
if it was God that made me move her, it was God

behind the bones, God in the hollowed throat, rising
like the spirit rising, like the flesh engorged,

hot, frantic with God—fat white child, the song
was in me. And the thought of the singing,

like the singing itself, taken whole, palpable
in its wholeness, no delicate "Jesus Loves Me" but "Lo!

Lord God Be in My Soul" and "Hallelujah!
the Song Is Risen in Me"—me, indelibly pale-eyed,

luminous in the midst of the dark singers.

                                       I would not be late.
My voice unfaltering, indistinguishable from the whole,

I would flow into them, roll on with them
and the God of the music would ascend with the words:
    "Hallelujah!

Hallelujah! and the song, Oh Lord, is risen in me."

II

Squat as a shed, the Assembly of God
sat like a stronghold on the flat, tamped earth between

the root beer stand and the white-fenced pasture
of horses; the acrid smell of bay salt mixed with the sweat

of the brown men who were always, even Sundays, working
the street. And predictable as the sweet-spoiled odor

of the defunct tannery by the landfill, little Jesús Manon-Diaz
watched the singers gather, perched every Sunday, alone

on the caved-in steps of the burned-out house on the corner.
He stared as though he himself were invisible, so earnestly

were his simple eyes fixed on the wide, open doors of the flat
white church. His Tijuana accent, thick as corn mush, carried
    "Jesus Loves

the Little Children" sweetly, even to my ear, to the swept-clean
        concrete
where the singers came together. His solemn brown child's face was
        empty,

and at the simplest gesture, from anyone at all, he would turn
and stop singing; on his belly, he would crawl beneath the lowest
        battened

two-by-four barring the doorway and then, after a small silence, his
        voice

would trickle like thin smoke from the glassless windows of his
    ruined cathedral.

He sang, ". . . all, Jesus, Jesus, all the little children of the world."

III

Calm as sand I took my place amidst the glorious bodies, glided onto
the smooth round edge of the pew, polished wood as heaven must
    have been glorious

and polished. Smack in God's lap, surrounded by elbows and the great
    wide hips
of the grandmas I chose to place myself among, I waited—their
    voices

would be the first to rise. And I knew the weightlessness
of anticipation, the accumulation of the waiting: the hymnal

weighed nothing, the pages turned like nothing, and then, when the
    salty glory
poured from the glistening faces, when the lively risen arms swayed
    side to side,

over the body of heads, far above my own lifted and undulating arms,
I was taken up; there was no tongue that did not sing in its way, no
    stilled

foot, no languorous arm. I was nestled in the center of believing—
belief residing in the stormy throats, the wild limbs and heartbeat
    footwork

of the singers. I was whole, I was one of many, I had no face, no past,
no present but the ascension of the song, and I sang, I sang for that

which surrounded me, for the glory it lent me—God's voice for the
    partaking—
and blinded and bodiless from the joy of such a song, I was swept
    away.

Eighty

I am eighty, surely I am
eighty, though my ticket to birth
states, unequivocally thirty-seven, thirty
and seven, the year forty-nine, and still
I am eighty, surely, born like any other
fat white baby, born like the juicy, irresponsible
pale and blue-eyed flesh I still am. Jesus,
God, it is important to get to eighty.

In order to be eighty, one must be
wise, I am told, wise, as they say, as
the sages. It is not true. I am eighty,
eighty in the marrow, eighty in that crucial
spot behind the eyes, eighty, eighty is old, but not
old. Eighty is too damn smart for one's own
salvation, too damn late, too compact, too much vital
information stored in the creases. Well,
then, eighty is not what I am. Eighty
is what I would be, if I could.

My mother is nearly eighty, then. My mother
who is the mainstay, the corset stay, the bone,
the ecru and folded, cut-on-the-bias silk night
dress, that mother is nearly eighty—she, round
as an apple, taller than I by one mere inch
or two and, don't you forget it, damn
proud of it. Some joke that. Some joke,
my mother at nearly eighty, slower, yes,
but kinder, fat as butter, and right
as only near-eighty can be, right hind-
sight, right miraculous, backwards and forwards
right, comprehension, applied, served with under-
standing and enough recognition to keep it to one's
self. Eighty.

Of All the Prints My Mother Sold
(Odalisque in Sepia)

I am sad that this is gone: browns like teas
and parchment, even the glass aged dark, the color of a smudge

and the cow in the foreground like a large brown
mottled stone grazing on brown grass, beneath the one

brown tree, the rising brown field at her thick back,
and in brown soil four hooves planted like more stones.

Photograph, 1962

In 1962, there was snow. It's still there,
shallow and gray in the photograph my mother

sends, the year tattooed in thick numbers pale
on the back, and on front: black and white

slightly out-of-focus confirmation of what I
had always suspected: me unsmiling, always

unsmiling, hair longer, thicker, darker, and body
bent double, scraping up my quadrant of snow

for the war, me in black knit pants, me fat in a cardigan
buttoned to the neck and pulled on backwards, me with the dark

boy across the street, five years my senior, Italian,
and jacketed up for the snow; he played "Twilight Time"

and made me fall in love with love the first
time. Somewhere behind the lens: my mother, always

my mother invisible behind the lens. I can't
recall what she wore in snow; no picture exists

of my mother, no image at all called 1962,
except the camera for her eye.

IV

Salt

The San Francisco Bay Region is one of the few areas in the world where salt is commercially recovered from brine by solar evaporation. The Bay itself provides the brine, and the mild climate provides favorable atmospheric conditions.

—Dedication Program, Wind-Powered Archimedes Screw
Pump, ASME/Leslie Salt Co., February 28, 1984

I

Whiter even than the skin of pale breasts
the salt pyramids pressed against the bluest sky—
always at the edge of the city and invisible
as your hand or your foot, the blindness that familiarity
breeds the way joy breeds joy, or ignorance
surprise. Rising in the midst of the fish boats,
the pleasure boats, the harbors like rings
on the fingers of the land: salt towers
like an eastern ridge, inevitable, invisible salt.

II

Everything was sex or engines. If you were fast,
if you had the drive, that was the place to go:
Evaporation Heaven, ponds like furrowed acres, the crust,
the salt, crisp as beach sand, crisper even. No one I knew
ever touched foot to pond. The story was like this:
the brine shrimp would rush with their numberless
tongues, burrow in your skin, countless infinitesimal wounds
laying your secretmost particles open to salt. You could die
from the pain. But back by the scaffoldlike loaders where the earth
held firm, out by the cranes and the carriers, the salt railroad
tripped along the shallow edges, and there your car
would careen, stuffed to bursting with adolescent flesh,
an hour to kill with the view and a taste for hot skin. Never

a plain horizon: you faced the mountains, or the salt. The cock
in your hand beat like a heart. You learned to make it in long,
husky Chevys—out there by the docks, beside the ponds, you
    watched
the salt like a sunset, watched the pools change color while the
    daylight
bled away, while the sun lingered in the opposite mountains, blue
    ponds,
red ponds, a thousand opalescent shades in between, and when the
    sun set
the billion stars tumbled onto the surface, stars white as salt far out
    in the wide-open bay.

III

The pilot on the bridge of the deep-water freighter spotted
Gavin Mickle's father, dead against the salt—a rag of a man
even when alive, at forty-two, and drying on the mound, they said
he seemed old as the sun. Everyone figured him gone on a bender,
    no one
thought to look; for two days he lay, leather burning in the salt.
For fifteen years he'd run track at the plant, a brittle man with a
    pregnant wife
and Gavin, his eldest, took after his dad: half his father's dying age,
his head's shot off in Vietnam. Here is how it started: the tightassed
young foreman, new to the ponds and a deacon at the white man's
    church,
canned Gavin's father in a rage against the drink—it wasn't true that
    day
but when the last shift ended, Mickle took himself up in the bucket
    scaffold rig,
laid himself upright on the wall that was salt, and the bullet took his
    brain
deep into the mound. Gavin took his father's job, and when the
    army took him
he was glad. He said it was the cycle of the Irish, of the young, of the
    salt. That's how it happened.

IV

You go because of the mare; you believe that. Fifth grade, sixth grade
you walk home the long way around, eight blocks to the Negro
     grocery
where, in good weather, you gingerly step over the owner's blind
     wife;
she sits in a chair on the sidewalk, her legs like dry stalks, her hair
     the color of dry
red peppers; you are convinced she knows the future. Three more
     blocks
and you pass the busted gas pumps where the boys hang out.
     Another block and you will see her,
the gray-white mare on Elm, the docile horse behind the white rail
     fence,
beside the stark white house with unbroken glass in the center of its
     wooden door,
the house with the shining upstairs windows, with the four great
     columns, thicker than men, that rise,
invulnerable, over the stairs you have never seen anyone climb. You
     save your apples;
you don't like them anyway. And you go. You walk off by yourself;
you are always by yourself; you drag your school bag over the cracks
in the gray cement where the earth has risen beneath, you drag it
     over the coarse ropes
of wild grass that rise between the irregular squares; the sound is
     like someone following.
The hem of your skirt is uneven; your shoes are thick and clumsy,
     your hair is lank. You are
as pale as poor light; you are better off with horses. So you go all that
     way
to touch the great, lean ears of the gray-white mare, to feel the thick
     down of her cavernous nostrils—
and it catches your eye, every time, it goads you like a sun: salt
     stone,
salt cake like a shoebox, lick heavy as a cinder block, salt carelessly
     thrown

in the high tufted grass, by the squat-legged bathtub filled with
    water for the mare.
You give her your apple; her lips are thick and soft, careful; her bone
    teeth
are the most powerful thing you know. You linger at the fence, one eye
on the glass of the blinding windows, the other on the eye of the
    mare—
a dark and seemingly endless eye, vast as you imagine the vastness
    of infinity.
You leave your books behind. You hang one leg, lop it over the white
    rung,
and duck in quickly. With your small hands, you press the bellow
    sides of the solid, lonesome horse
and move in, bend low, your ridiculous skirt climbing the backs of
    your legs.
You rest, crouched beneath the overwhelming belly of the gentle
    mare; you touch your tongue to the salt.

V

OK, I'll tell the truth: it was never a stranger. Julio Martin
broke down that door. It wasn't the first time. I thought
my life was over: a rolling drunk, wet, sloppy at the mouth,
wild and blind at the same time, his dark eyes dull as tobacco,
his slick skin like dark wood, distortion rode him like an animal,
    anger
like a skin on his body. He took my long hair, it was nothing
in his hand, came loose in his fist, he tore my eye. The first time
he saw he could hurt me he said: she deserves it, she begs for it, God,
she is not a good girl, she's bad, she's poison, and he knew I would
    never tell:
he left slowly, he smiled, the moon-faced son-of-a-bitch, my brother,
    and left only his dark,
sour smell behind. That last time, I had the gun, our own mother
    gave me
the oily gun, but, before I could get to it, he had me on the fresh-
    made bed,

had me on my narrow white sheets, his long, barrel body covered
    mine like a skin.
But I am the daughter of Cornelia Martin, daughter of Juan, and God
    showed him
a sister's got a right, Lina Rosamonde has a right: his eyes turned up
    before
he could get it in, he dropped in the swamp of his sweat, something
    went wrong
in his brain, blew the slippery cells apart, his body was like no
    weight
I could explain, like a full barrel gone soft; above me he sighed
    himself empty
like a death-throe dog, spilt the bitter piss like a foul, shallow bay,
    like
a low-tide bay. I could smell the shit. I breathed the salt sweat, the
    salt spit; this time
it was my freedom. They burned him in South City where our father
    was burned,
and Mama put his ashes on the window ledge. I leave the window
    open. I still keep the gun.

VI

She has studied the man in the moon, knows his rampant features
through the braille of light and dark; she knows his name.
She is mute, her bones the bones of small night animals, and she
    does not know how she came there,
but from where she stands on the mountain, his face is clear, his
    need
plain: she is the moon's old servant, gray woman as mad as the tides.
The sea boils; she can smell it, rising, invisible in the west, pungent
as pepper. The wind braids her hair; she is not conscious of the cold.
Planted on the stone, she faces the ludicrous moon. When her body
    fails,
when in her weakness she turns east where the warm lights burn,
    scattered like asters below her,
she sees the salt, small mounds in that distance, blue in the
    lessening

light; the moon behind her, she believes she can hear the wheeze of
    the trolley,
she believes the scaffold lights flicker, eclipsed and then passed by,
    and she does not know
how she comes to know such a far-off place. The moon at her narrow
    back,
and still as the mountain beneath her, she hums softly to the glis-
    tening edge of her faint earth.